UPCYCLED

POETRY REPURPOSED

UPCYCLED
POETRY REPURPOSED

by

Andi Penner

Mercury HeartLink
www.HeartLink.com

Upcycled

ISBN 978--1-949652-33-8
Publisher Mercury HeartLink
Silver City, New Mexico
Printed in the United States of America

Front Cover image: La Poeta by Jade Leyva
www.jadeleyvaart.com

Author photo by Meg Leonard 2017

Layout and cover design by Pamela Warren Williams

Author contact: pennerink@gmail.com

Mercury HeartLink: consult@heartlink.com

For Keith, my long tall drink of water for the last twenty-three years.

Foreword

Upcycled is a wonderful collection of poems that feels in balance with the earth and the natural cycle of life, far more than any I have read in recent years. It is filled with playful language that surprises and delights, alongside deep ideas, rooted in the earth and our place on it. Lineage in this chapbook is handled in a complex and compelling way.

There are so many chapbooks that simply praise nature, and others that bemoan the state of the natural world, and what humans have done to it. *Upcycled* manages to capture both praise and worry, the unknown future a source of tension, pulling the poet and the reader forward.

I am grateful to have spent time with these pages.

~Caitlin Elizabeth Jans
Founding Editor, Authors Publish Magazine
Co-founder of The Poetry Marathon
Toronto, Canada

Contents

an assemblage of words
like 'white' and 'bones'
'sticks & stones'
folded scraps of unlocked paper memory

–Julie Suzanne Brökken

bricolage, n.
The manner or practice of creating art and poetry from varied, miscellaneous materials already in existence.

Preface

In this life-moment, I am both bricoleur and recycler of my sixty-five years on the planet, transforming the material of my life, including old poems, for the present moment.

My writing can be found in lit mags, libraries, and landfills. It has been crumpled and composted, burned to ash and restored as art. And in the process, I have grown as a writer.

Given the odds—i.e., my grandmothers were centenarians (100 and 108, respectively)—I am entering the final third of my life; however, as a cancer survivor whose mother died of a rare disease at age 75, I know better than to assume longevity.

This little book exists in your hands because if not now, when?

Andi Penner
Albuquerque, New Mexico
Summer 2024

Indicates revised, improved, and upcycled versions of poems published in one of my books, *When East Was North* (2012) or *Rabbit Sun, Lotus Moon* (2017).

Go into All the World

after "Witness" by Denise Levertov

She watches from her kitchen window
whenever the mesas hide themselves
behind a gray summer mantle,
its hem caught on the desert

floor. As the light returns, she turns away,
stirs a pot of fragrant stew—maybe mutton,
maybe beef, some salt—relieved
to hide inside herself, for now.

God knows she believes the gospel,
the choice to serve, bear witness,
but sometimes when the baby sleeps,
when her husband preaches in the stone church,

she feels watched by the holy ones—
the sacred many who live in clouds,
in mountains. The ones who ask her

why she came.

Note from a student

I read your poems last night.
Then I went to a class....

Life **S**kills

The letter S never
never seemed
more important.

Agency

You may bury me under the chocolate flower*
scatter me to the sea
lower me into loamy earth
covered with aspen leaves

sift me with the sand of a southern shore
float me on a twig in the creek
hold me up to the arctic wind
blowing down from the highest peak

and I'll traverse the midnight sky
find silence among the stars
my arms enfolding galaxies
a universe expanding my heart.

So bury me under the chocolate flower
or scatter me to the sea,
but release me from your notions

of eternity.

*Yellow chocolate flowers grow wild in the dry altitude of New Mexico. And yes, the brown center bears the scent of chocolate. Heavenly.

In the Desert Southwest, Rain Is a Countable Noun

charged particles
arouse thunder

clouds tease
the sun

gray lace veils
descend
to meet
the dusty
horizon

drops fall
one by one

by none

Camino de Los Abuelos

That paved road
from Eldorado to Madrid
bends by Old Galisteo Church,
dips at a Watch for Water
sign that seldom delivers
on its promise.

At Cemetery Hill,
the road divides history
Catholic   Protestant.
Stone walls and locked
gates protect prairie dogs
and plastic flowers.
Saints and sinners
share a withered faith.

Asphalt undulates west
across arid basins, curves
north toward mountain snow,
and slithers south, striking
indigo bootheels. Abandoned
mines protect old stories
only the crows remember.

Taste the Morning

Love is the soul's light, the taste of morning
~Jalal ad-Din Muhammad Rumi

Summer sunrise responds
to coyote song. Your lover
sleeps, one with lace shadows
on torso-twisted sheets.

You inhale the barest hint of fall
and you pray—Not yet—
we are made for pleasure, for
hot days and sweaty nights.

Wake up, my love. Drink the light
of morning ritual. Day's yellow dress
caresses earth's brown body. Let
the sun have its way with us.

Slake this thirst for love. Suck sweet
grape pulp from bitter cuticle. Devour
ripe flesh, seed, soul together.

Reflection

Foothill seclusion
above sleeping city
tea-kettle companion
purrs
gas flame
glows
blue lotus
opens
to ascending

moon

to ascend
open
blue lotus
glow
flame
purr
my companion
asleep

Aging in Tree Pose

The endless yellow canopy
of cottonwoods in the bosque

salutes the sun
in a cloudless sky.

Where the male poet saw
the withered crotch of trees,

I see riparian elders dressed
for autumn, sisters

balanced on scarred trunks
held by riverine roots,

mature abundant boughs
embracing. I want to age

brilliant and serene

necklaced for spring
in ruby catkins

adorned for fall
in gold.

When the Wind Blows

Indeed, the very hairs of your head are all numbered. Don't be afraid;
you are worth more than many sparrows.
~Luke 12:7

A basket-home
under my juniper tree—
tiny broken shell
clinging to its nursery.

I cradle the nest
and see
            not God,
but sparrows count
as worthy the hairs
of my head—
gray-brown curls
woven with twigs
and colored thread.

The School-Year Begins

Lovers greet the dying sun,
claim the evening star.

Teens smoke cigarettes
in their friend's car.

Kids chase the veteran riding
with a parrot on the handlebar.

Parents watch the nightly
news of another war.

A woman stops ironing
    mid-collar
military portraits as
bodies are identified
and names, known—
age [too young], rank,
and home town.

She is every mother;
her child, every soldier.

IF

Some
days I
slow my steps
right down to
rub rosemary,
snap sage,
pocket a nickel,
or
glance
at a
handsome
man.

Might
miss
him
if I
walk
too
fast.

Peril

Earth eclipses her
sun, tips her hat
to the moon and stars
and waves

rides currents and
comets' tails

gathers flesh
scatters bone
spins seasons
                into straw

turns ice to fire
fire to glass
in white sand

which we ignore

and drag the net
hauling her beauty
to shore

How Could This Be?

The morning beauty
was absurd—
beauty around me
beauty before me.

A flock of sky-sheep
above turquoise mountain.
Wizened grandfather toad
and two-spirit butterflies.

Your son would have
known their stories
because you taught him well.

He grew in *hozho*.
He grew in *sihasin*.
He grew in beauty.
He grew in love.

Mourning doves
in piñon, in juniper
and cicada wings
gone silent.

Love on the Road

Yesterday began with a lunar eclipse
obscured by clouds, or so you told me
when you touched my cheek,
handed me a paper cup of motel coffee
and said, *I hate to wake you, but....*

Mouths watering for New Mexico
chile, we drove through sleepy T or C
past teal and flamingo bath houses,
searching for breakfast cafes, but
even the OPEN places were closed.

In Hatch, we found E & J's—
a five-table kitchen, gregarious hosts.

"You never been here, before?!" said E
as we turned our coffee cups right-side up.
"Just about everybody but Obama's
been through here," he said, naming
a dozen politicians.

"These are hot," said J, and we knew she
meant both plates and chile: tortillas, eggs,
and beans smothered with Christmas,
red and green.

E soap-boxed about his crops
and water rights and Denver idiots
who complain about his little salsa-
bottling business. We bought a jar.

Southward, more poems—
ditches and dairies
vineyards and wineries.
We crossed flat openness
to Nutt, Deming, Uvas…
St. Clair and Luna Rossa—
blood moon, I wrote.

We consumed Mimbres history,
asked for a map at Faywood,
picnicked in City of Rocks—
state park rangers stern as
border patrol. Kneeling Nun
mourned her sisters
laid bare in Santa Rita
Copper Mine.

Fire-scarred mountain wilderness
over Emory Pass—
historical marker,
early scientific survey;
passed through Kingston and Hillsboro,
too tired to stop. Back in T or C
we bathe in rising steam.

Luminarias*

Late afternoon tea—
a slice of moon on desert toast
served with prickly pear.

~

Reach for azure sky
draw river ink through dry veins
calligraphy the shore.

~

Curled under moonrise
shivering mice
fear owl's penumbra.

~

Desert willow blooms.
Magenta trumpet orchids
herald monsoon rain.

~

Sturdy Mormon tea—
steeped, knock-kneed stems
sustenance of saints.

*__Little lights__. These poems once appeared as *weathergrams*—
poems calligraphed on strips of brown paper hung in trees.

Chocolate is Predictable, War is Obvious

after Susan Sontag

What I like: Dog-eared paperbacks, homemade rice custard, waves crashing, obsidian, knowing names of Premier League footballers, bay windows, wool, handwritten letters, apricots, the word languid, blue gates, afternoon naps in the sun, textiles and tapestry, paths, the sound of migrating geese, adagios.

~

What I dislike: Canned peas, statements posed as questions, the outfield, family secrets, ice water in winter, mold (except in bleu cheese), parsimony, horror films, artificial turf, nausea, sloppy editing, small talk, Velcro, when I procrastinate, wasps, excuses, tyrants.

First Blush

All praise
to the sun, the rain
last winter's snow
and someone's
thought
long ago
to plant
this rose.

All gratitude
for hands (not
mine) that
nurtured
root stock
vine.

All joy
inside this heart
intoxicated,
by scarlet petals
and rare perfume.

May It Please Superior Court*

Their favorite color is blue.
Eyes, soft as a lazuli bunting.
Blue, like the mountains of Santa Cruz
on late evening drives, blue
highway wending down through
redwood forests to the green-
blue sea. Watery sky, sublime
Paris blue. Fluid boundary
birthing ocean, cloud.

California blue, they tell you. Indigo,
sung by midnight saxes, transposed
sapphires. You know—piano vibes.
Not your seventies' Joni album,
Blue. Stripe of harmony in rainbow
flags—fly yours! Androgynous, like
spiky hair, bubblegum, and recycled 501s.
Non-binary blue, eighteen candles tall,
legal birthday, turquoise pride takes the cake.

Petition granted. Make a wish, Blue.

*Legal name changes in California require a court petition. Our grandchild, who goes by Blue, will soon be eighteen.

Perspective

Unlike the notorious
water glass

the moon
is never

    half empty.

My Step-Mother Was Born Near Hiroshima

Five cranes fly overhead
that April day in 'twenty-nine,
auspicious beginning for
unlucky girl
whose mother died
and father vanished.

Neighbors take her, keep her in
a house of wives and mistresses.
Silk kimonos in their closets—
cotton rags in hers.

Tiny cranes she folds
from paper scraps,
tucks beneath tatami.
Cold nights she frees them one
by one on frosted breath.

Fifteen when firestorms
begin. Sixteen
when they, when we,
drop the bomb
above her creased
creations.

One day she, too
will fly, miscarry
twice,
and marry
for love.

Shootin' Pool

a New Orleans sestina for Kendall Williams

Two twenty-two. Afternoon deadlock at White
and Washington. Sirens scrape Thirteenth's daylight.
Death goads life, *Call it*. Chalk it up to violent
no-excuse-for-it sidewalk crime near the Broad Street
strip mall. Divine Hands Hair Salon, Video City,
and Kajun Crab can't keep young men racked-up, safe.

Unidentified somebody's son pops the Glock's safety,
shoots stripes and solids, and slips cops' black-and-whites.
Victim, twenty-to-one clean shot at life in the chocolate city,
on the ball, survived the flood, his family's plight,
federal so-called assistance. In the kitchen, off the street,
he catches a break along the rail, but violence

runs the ball, breaks the triangle, violates
the felt. Ghost-ball jumps the table, angles safely
to a corner pocket of narrow streets,
glances the sidewalk, and rolls past white
do-gooders mapping post-Katrina blight,
abandoned homes, and parish cities.

                                        Department duplicity
breaks the po'boy, *beignet,* voodoo spell and violence
pockets the change. Red-blue-white guardian angel lights
pursue the perp, but scratch the table. No fail-safe
after two—now three—murders near White
and Washington's indifferent. Up to Eden Street,

down Eve, traffic slows for detour arrows, street
signs. Shotgun-shack and crawfish city
curious—black and brown, rainbow and white—
rue their brother's chalk outline, own 'hoods violated.
There ain't no such thing as gun safety,
baby girl. Damn. Curse the devils' sleight

of hand, red sedans cruising through stoplights
on Thirteenth, Fourteenth, Sixteenth ward backstreets
halfway to homicide. Every quarter declares safety
before the next shots carom against a city
crescent inured to violence
and pools cash for a second-line parade, off-white

marble, and white *fleur-de-lis.* Safe home, interred?
Violence deterred? Steady light rain on city streets.

Note: On the day of the murder, March 4, 2013, I was with my twenty-five-year-old son at his Green Coast recovery office in post-Katrina New Orleans, in the Broadmoor neighborhood. We heard gunshots. My son ran toward the commotion, telling me to stay inside. The victim, Kendall Williams, just a few years younger than my son, died that day at Washington and White, a few blocks away. I started writing the poem that night in my journal.

Summer Sunday on the Rio Grande

Old luck spills
from a half-drunk horseshoe
onto a rusted wreath, a
            crown of barbed wire
            cinched with brackets,
            laced with lavender ghost bundles.

A warped ladder leans
against cracked adobe.
            Mud-wall menders
            gather, mañana.

Ristras—sun-dried garlic and red chile—
sag from twine skeletons, love-tied
by forgotten hands. Abandoned
honeycomb racks frame silence.

Someone has watered here.   Droplets
cling to corn, squash, and beans—
trinity of fecund sisters pulsing with xylem—
living sacraments
            more resilient than priests' vineyards,
            more nourishing than broken bread.

Where do you worship?

    In the garden where I know,
    am known.

Pomegranates dangle
like upside-down Cochiti ollas and Tesuque jars,
calyxed husks glazed gold and crimson.
Chambers of fleshy sarcotesta
protect vermillion seeds.

Roots time-travel into history's sediment.
Geese alight in alfalfa, feed,
preen, and fly again, north across West
Mesa's buried bones.   Our open space rolls
    down and up this grand trickle of river,
    desert artery where people dance
    and drum. We have come
    hungry. Ripe
for rain.

Writer's Asana

I write
short, loose lines
or my hand goes numb.

I write in color
and shadow—
snapshot memories
for Anne Lamott's
one-inch picture
frame.

I write myself
into a corner
with nowhere
else to go
and write
myself out
again.

I write flannel nights and
denim afternoons
I write the lost years
with an unquiet mind
in child's pose.

Fair Share

Apolitical, but intuitive, Mom redistributed chocolate chips equitably before sliding baking sheets into the oven. When they were done, she served us kids and our friends the same number of cookies on each plate, but almost always granted seconds. From her I learned about fairness and generosity.

Staying with me to help after the birth of my second child, mom offered to indulge me with a healthy dessert full of whole wheat bread, eggs, milk, cinnamon, grated apple, and, of course, raisins. We chatted quietly while she stirred ingredients and I nursed my son. The longer he suckled, the hungrier I became. By the time he fell asleep in my arms, I was ravenous, but Mom was absently planting raisins in the unbaked bread pudding.

DÉJÀ VU [2016, 2020]

eleven nineteen…
twelve thirty-six…
two ten
restless winds
ravage, roar, repeat
one awake one asleep
curve of hip slope of thigh
one wondering, how the hell?
one dreaming, kill the rattlesnake

thunder rattles lightning
strikes, rattlesnake strikes
teachers strike more pay, equal pay
snakes won't ratify the naked
truth that women are equal
men suffer, too, mounting lies
lying under mountains
burning
curve of flesh slope of hip
three twenty-seven, twenty-eight
red digits add to zero tolerance
for promises to America
best left un-made

Emily's Winter Aftermath of Grief

Before the ground has frozen
'neath winter's snow and ice
soil will envelope me—
a quiet burial, suffice.

Forgotten, but not gone.

Rest in compost
roots forlorn, dark months
alone my soul
seeks solitude.

Remember me—
help me remember
how to swell
rupture, thrive.

Rabbit Sun

Mammatus clouds
hang heavy

rabbit hides from hawks
chamisa to rock to cactus
twitches and listens
sniffs deer tracks

snowflakes flit
one here one there
as morning fireflies

white-winged ice fairies
dance on Apache plume
disappear in shadows

we hold each other tight
praying the sun will stay
                    one step
ahead of winter

CHEMO*

A child's round balloon
Floating wishes—"Get Well Soon!"
Daddy's love, let go.

~

Cumulus clouds build
snowlike mountains to the north.
My heart travels south.

~

Haiku are good for
cancer. I can still count to
five and to seven.

~

Infusion chatter
Nurses laugh. Monitors chime
beep...beep...toodle-loo!

~

Celebrate all six
achieving halfway to twelve—
chocolate power.

* I wrote these haiku while in the infusion chair at the cancer center, notable only because it made me happy that even with chemo brain, I could still count syllables.

He's the Only One Who Calls Me "And"

Rebuild.
Days after the dream,
I called.

Hi, And! he answered on the fourth ring.
(Only my brother calls me "&.")
Let me put you on speaker, he said.
I heard him whisk something in a bowl.
What's for dinner, Jeff?
Meatballs, but not Mom's recipe, he said.

We traded stories about rain in California
and drought in New Mexico. About
his job, my job, words, and books
we're reading. He said,
I still haven't read *Brothers Karamazov*
(our Dad's favorite Russian novel).
There's still time, I said.

We talked about his kidneys
(thus no-salt meatballs).
I said, "have to wake up early tomorrow."

Choose.
I hesitated. Maybe he hasn't thought much

about hereditary cancer.

Build.
I laid out the medical blueprint—
second mammogram, ultrasound, biopsy.
He surprised me by asking,
How do you feel about more tests?

Breathe.
I've hit the emotional floor, I said.
Even though it's routine, even though
it's probably nothing, even though only
twenty percent of breast biopsies
are positive… but there's the gene.

Then I told him about my dream….
A wildfire, smoke,
our house destroyed
we weren't ready
someone questioned me
Do you want them to use glue
or build it new?

I told him I heard myself choose
build it new.

Call us tomorrow. And, he said,
I love you.

The Poet in New Orleans

She and a stranger,
about her son's age,
wait outside at MSY.

He: Are you coming home or visiting?
(Sips his airport Hurricane. Second? Third?)

She: Visiting my son.

He: I was just in New York visiting my mother.
It got a little tense, but it was good. Yeah.
There's just somethin' tender between
a mother and son. You know?
I'm sure you do your fucking best.
(Drains his cocktail glass.) You do
the best you can for your children,
you know, and then, fuck 'em.

His ride drives a black Mercedes.
The poet opens her notebook—
too good not to quote
for future use.

August Blessing, Year-Round

Eight stanzas, thirty-one words

Sunlight
awaken you

Cumulous clouds
befriend you

Roadside sunflowers
guide you

Female rain
save you

Twilight
cleanse you

Starry sky
soothe you

Dawn
restore you

Earth love
and keep you
safe

Acknowledgments

Many thanks and much love to poet-friends, poetry-teachers, and poem-appreciators. Special thanks to Pamela Warren Williams who encouraged and designed this work into being.

Upcycled comprises revised versions of many poems that debuted in either *When East Was North* (2012) or *Rabbit Sun, Lotus Moon* (2017)—both published by Mercury HeartLink—while others appeared first in *Fixed and Free* anthologies or assorted chapbooks.

I gratefully acknowledge the literary magazine editors who selected some of my newest work from among many submissions to include in their publications:

"Chocolate is Predictable, War is Obvious," *Flora and Fauna*, 2023
"Fair Share," *Dead Housekeeping*, 2016
"First Blush," *Women Raise Our Voices*, 2023
"Go into All the World," *Untold Volumes*, 2024
"May It Please Superior Court," *Does It Have Pockets?* 2024
"My Step-Mother Was Born Near Hiroshima," *Neologism*, 2023
"Shootin' Pool," *Kelsay Books Blog*, 2023
"Summer Sunday on the Rio Grande," *Sky Island Journal,* Issue 27, 2024

The Cover: Magical Realism Artist Jade Leyva is from Mexico City, living in New Mexico since 2006. Her work expresses her love of nature and her positive hope for the future of the world. She has participated in collective exhibitions at the local, national and international levels and her work is collected globally. Her work has included multi-year community artistic environmental awareness projects. For more information: jadeleyvaart.com

About the Author

Andrea (Andi) Penner lives and writes in Albuquerque, New Mexico, a traditional Tiwa homeland. Her poetry, a fan fave at open mics, has been published in anthologies and literary magazines. Her second book, *Rabbit Sun, Lotus Moon* (Mercury HeartLink, 2017), was an Arizona/New Mexico book award finalist in poetry. Andi is currently revising her memoir, which chronicles her transformative journey from Jewish teenager to Christian adult; from the physical and cultural landscape of southern California to the Navajo Nation; and from a woman in danger of losing herself into a woman of agency. You can read more of her poetry and prose on *In Our Own Ink*, andipenner.substack.com.

Photo credit: Meg Leonard,
megleonard.com

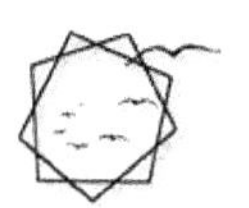

www.ingramcontent.com/pod-product-compliance
Lightning Source LLC
LaVergne TN
LVHW010108110826
845155LV00028B/540

* 9 7 8 1 9 4 9 6 5 2 3 3 8 *